The unabashed Alex

The unabashed Alex

Penguin Books

Published by the Penguin Group
27 Wrights Lane, London W8 5TZ, England
Viking Penguin Inc., 40 West 23rd Street, New York, New York
10010, USA
Penguin Books Australia Ltd, Ringwood, Victoria, Australia
Penguin Books Canada Ltd, 2801 John Street, Markham, Ontario,
Canada L3R 1B4
Penguin Books (NZ) Ltd, 182-190 Wairau Road, Auckland 10,
New Zealand
Penguin Books Ltd, Registered Offices: Harmondsworth,
Middlesex, England

These cartoon strips appeared first in the *Independent*
This collection first published in Penguin Books 1988
5 7 9 10 8 6 4

Made and printed in Great Britain by
Richard Clay Ltd, Bungay, Suffolk

Alex
PEATTIE + TAYLOR

YOU KNOW, GAVIN'S ONE OF THOSE FRANK, OPEN, HONEST PEOPLE SO RARE TODAY... IF HE'S GOT SOMETHING ON HIS MIND HE'LL JUST COME STRAIGHT OUT WITH IT...

..AND HE'S SO LIVELY, TALKATIVE AND GREGARIOUS...ALWAYS THE LIFE AND SOUL OF THE PARTY...

...BUT MOST OF ALL, HE'S A TRUE FRIEND. HE'S THE SORT OF PERSON WHO'LL PUT HIS FRIENDS BEFORE ANYTHING AND WOULD DO ANYTHING FOR THEM...

HOW DID THE INTERVIEW WITH THE MAN FROM THE MINISTRY GO ABOUT GAVIN'S CIVIL SERVICE POSITIVE VETTING?

EXCELLENT... I REALLY DROPPED HIM IN IT.

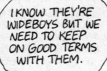

Alex
PEATTIE + TAYLOR

OH CLIVE, WE'RE MEETING THE MONEYBROKERS FROM METROBANK AFTER WORK...

I KNOW THEY'RE WIDEBOYS BUT WE NEED TO KEEP ON GOOD TERMS WITH THEM.

OH DEAR. I HOPE THEY DON'T ORDER CHAMPAGNE... IT ALWAYS MAKES ME SO GIGGLY...

ER... GARSON. WE'LL START WIV A BOTTLE OF MOWAY 'N' SHANDON...

SHHH.

TITTER TITTER

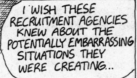

THE CRASH OF '87...

Alex PEATTIE + TAYLOR

LOOK ALL I CAN DO IS REPEAT WHAT I TOLD YOU YESTERDAY AND STATE QUITE CATEGORICALLY THAT OUR BANK IS NOT IN ANY SORT OF FINANCIAL TROUBLE...

WE HAVE EXPERIENCED SMALL LOSSES IN OUR INVESTMENT OPERATIONS, BUT NOTHING SIGNIFICANT. AS FOR MY OWN POSITION IN THE BANK I CAN ONLY REITERATE, IT IS ABSOLUTELY SECURE. HAVE YOU GOT THAT?

IT'S AT TIMES LIKE THIS THAT I REALLY REGRET HAVING GIVEN OUT MY DIRECT LINE NUMBER TO CERTAIN PEOPLE...

MOTHERS CAN'T HELP WORRYING, CLIVE.

Alex PEATTIE + TAYLOR

I SUPPOSE ALL OF US IN THE CITY HAVE BEEN TAKING THINGS FOR GRANTED FOR A LONG TIME...

AND NOW WE'RE ALL GOING TO HAVE TO REAPPRAISE OUR ATTITUDES TO SO-CALLED YUPPIE LIFESTYLES AND THE VALUES WE WERE SO SURE OF...

I MEAN, PEOPLE I KNOW ARE LOSING THEIR JOBS, HAVING TO SELL THEIR FLATS AND TRADING IN THEIR CARS...

NOW WHO KNOWS WHAT KIND OF PERSON MIGHT BE SEEN DRIVING ABOUT IN A 2ND HAND D. REG. B.M.W?

IT'S FRIGHTENING.

Alex PEATTIE + TAYLOR

ANOTHER STORY HERE ABOUT A TWELVE YEAR OLD SCHOOLBOY WHO WAS DABBLING IN THE STOCKMARKET.

BY ARRANGING CREDIT FROM FINANCIAL INSTITUTIONS HE MANAGED TO BUILD UP £300,000 WORTH OF SHARES.

AND THEN GOT WIPED OUT BY THE CRASH?

NO. HE SWAPPED THEM WITH A FRIEND FOR A SEVENTY-NINER CONKER AND A MASTERS-OF-THE-UNIVERSE ASSAULT ZOID.

Alex PEATTIE + TAYLOR

ROGER'S REALLY DEVASTATED ABOUT LOSING HIS JOB BECAUSE OF THE CRASH. HE'S HAD TO SELL HIS PORSCHE AND EVERYTHING...

HE SAYS IF HE CAN'T FIND WORK IN THE CITY AGAIN HE'S FINISHED - FIVE YEARS OF HIS CAREER DOWN THE DRAIN...

LIKE A LOT OF OTHERS HE'S SUDDENLY REALISED THAT HIS SPECIALISED SKILLS ARE TOTALLY USELESS OUTSIDE THE ARTIFICIAL ENVIRONMENT OF THE CITY...

I SUPPOSE IT'S TRUE...

THERE PROBABLY ISN'T A GREAT DEMAND FOR AVOCADO AND FOIS GRAS BAPS IN THE REAL WORLD...

Alex PEATTIE + TAYLOR

SQUASH COURTS

DON'T YOU THINK YOU'RE GOING A BIT OVER THE TOP, ALEX? AFTER ALL IT'S ONLY A GAME...

IT'S WORTH GOING TO A BIT OF TROUBLE TO IMPRESS YOUR OPPONENT WITH YOUR PROFESSIONALISM, CLIVE.

IT'S VERY IMPORTANT TO PSYCHE HIM OUT IN ADVANCE...

WHEN DO YOU PLAY HIM?

SPECTATORS GALLERY

THURSDAY WEEK.

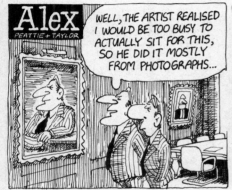

Alex PEATTIE + TAYLOR

COME ON, ALEX, YOU'RE THE ONE WHO WANTED TO GO TO THE THEATRE TONIGHT AND NOW YOU'RE MAKING US LATE.

I CAN'T FIND MY AMEX CARD, PENNY.

Peattie

BUT ALEX YOU'VE GOT YOUR ACCESS CARD AND YOUR VISA CARD AND ALL YOUR CHARGE CARDS.

AH! HERE IT IS.

...AND I'VE GOT MY DINERS CLUB CARD... BUT ONLY £80 IN CASH. REMIND ME TO STOP AT A CASHPOINT ON THE WAY...

...NOW IF I MAY HAVE A GENTLEMAN VOLUNTEER FROM THE AUDIENCE, I SHALL USE MY MENTAL POWERS TO DIVINE THE CONTENTS OF HIS WALLET...

Alex
PEATTIE + TAYLOR

ALEX IS ALWAYS HIRING THESE INCREDIBLY VIOLENT AMERICAN COP THRILLERS AND WAR MOVIES FROM THE VIDEO SHOP AND WATCHING THEM OBSESSIVELY OVER AND OVER AGAIN...

I DON'T LIKE THE IMPLICATIONS OF ALL THAT VOYEURISTIC SADISM. IT'S ALREADY STARTED TO HAVE AN UNNATURAL EFFECT ON HIS BEHAVIOUR, ESPECIALLY IN BED.

YOU KNOW, HE WENT INTO A SEX SHOP LAST WEEK AND ORDERED A FULL-LENGTH CEILING MIRROR FOR THE BEDROOM...

EUR... HOW HORRID!

THIS BIT'S BRILLIANT WHERE HE WASTES THIS MONASTERY WITH A ROCKET-LAUNCHER.

Alex PEATTIE + TAYLOR

CLIVE, I'M RATHER BUSY... WOULD YOU MIND TAKING MR BOGISS FROM ARKON OIL OUT TO LUNCH?

OH NO, ALEX, NOT AFTER THE LAST CLIENT YOU DUMPED ON ME. HE WAS WEARING BROWN SHOES AND WHITE SOCKS AND A KIPPER TIE AND A MAUVE SHIRT AND IT WAS REALLY EMBARRASSING HAVING TO SIT IN THE RESTAURANT WITH HIM.

I ASSURE YOU, CLIVE, HE'LL BE WEARING A BLUE SUIT AND BLACK SHOES. HE'S PERFECTLY PRESENTABLE, JUST RATHER ENTHUSIASTIC ABOUT FOSSIL FUELS...

OH ALRIGHT.

NOW, CLIVE LAD, YOU'D BE AMAZED AT THE THINGS WE CAN DERIVE FROM OIL: TAKE MY SHIRT: POLYESTER! AND MY SHOES: PLASTIC WOULD YOU BELIEVE?! MY SOCKS: NYLON!...

WHAT'S THE PLAT DU JOUR?

DISH OF THE DAY IN FRENCH, SIR.

PASS THE PORTABLE TELEPHONE.

Alex PEATTIE + TAYLOR

ALEX CAN BE SO EMBARRASSING AT THESE PARTIES IF HE SEES ME TALKING TO OTHER MEN...

I MEAN, I'M NOT HIS PROPERTY. I DON'T SEE WHY HE SHOULD MAKE SUCH A FUSS...

JUST BECAUSE HE FOUND OUT THAT SOME PERFECTLY NICE GENTLEMAN HAD INVITED ME OUT TO LUNCH NEXT WEEK — HIS REACTION HAS BEEN ABSURD.

YOU'D HAVE THOUGHT HE'D HAVE SHUT UP ABOUT IT BY NOW...

AND APPARENTLY HE WAS THE VICE PRESIDENT OF CREDIT ZURICH WITH HIS OWN PRIVATE JET...

GOSH.

Alex PEATTIE + TAYLOR

I FEEL DREADFUL... THIS IS WORSE THAN I EXPECTED.

I KNOW IT'S A BIT ROUGH

BUT IT'S ONLY A SHORT FLIGHT.

I'M REALLY SORRY, CLIVE... THIS IS SO EMBARRASSING. I THINK I'M GOING TO HAVE TO AVAIL MYSELF OF THE SICKBAG...

NO NEED TO APOLOGISE, ALEX.

I THINK YOU'RE DOING JOLLY WELL, CONSIDERING THIS IS THE FIRST TIME YOU'VE TRAVELLED ECONOMY CLASS.

I'LL NEVER LIVE THIS DOWN...

Alex
PEATTIE + TAYLOR

I FIND IT HARD TO BELIEVE YOU EVER WORE CLOTHES LIKE THAT, ALEX...

OH YES. LEATHER JACKET, DRAINPIPE JEANS, GREASED BACK HAIR...

I SUPPOSE I WAS DISASSOCIATING MYSELF FROM THE ESTABLISHMENT AND MY BACKGROUND. I WANTED TO PROJECT A MORE STREET CREDIBLE IMAGE AT THAT TIME. ANYWAY IT WAS ALL QUITE SHORT-LIVED...

SO WHAT HAPPENED?

WELL, THE DEFENDANT DIDN'T OBJECT TO ME AS A JURYMAN AND ON THE SECOND DAY OF MY JURY SERVICE I CHANGED BACK INTO MY SUIT AND FOUND HIM GUILTY.

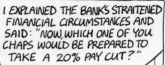

Alex
PEATTIE + TAYLOR

DID YOU PLAY ANY GOLF WHEN YOU WERE OUT IN JAPAN?

YOU'RE JOKING. IT'S INCREDIBLY EXPENSIVE. CLUB FEES ALONE ARE LITERALLY ¼ OF A MILLION QUID.

ALL THE BANK'S EMPLOYEES USED TO GO TO THESE SPECIAL INDOOR GOLF SCHOOLS, FANTASISING ABOUT THE DAY THEY MIGHT GET TO PLAY ON A REAL GOLF COURSE...

ON THE OFF-CHANCE THAT ONE DAY THEY MIGHT BE INVITED TO PLAY A ROUND WITH THE BOSS, THEY DEDICATE YEARS TO PRACTISING ALL THE NECESSARY SKILLS...

LIKE WHAT?

HOW TO SLICE A DRIVE; HOW TO PLAY A LOFT SHOT INTO A BUNKER FROM ANY PART OF THE FAIRWAY; HOW TO MISS A SIX-INCH PUTT CONVINCINGLY...

KERCHUNG.

Alex
PEATTIE + TAYLOR

OH NO. LOOK WHAT MY GRANDFATHER HAS SENT ME FOR MY BIRTHDAY. A REVOLTING CHEAP LITTLE PLASTIC CIGARETTE LIGHTER.

WHAT ON EARTH HAS GOT INTO HIM? EVERY YEAR FOR THE PAST TEN YEARS HE'S SENT ME A CRISP NEW £5 NOTE...

BUT YOU ALWAYS COMPLAIN WHEN HE SENDS YOU A FIVER, ALEX. SO WHAT'S THE DIFFERENCE?

LOOK, PENNY, EVERY YEAR ON MY BIRTHDAY WE GO OUT FOR A BIG MEAL WITH FRIENDS, AND AT THE END OF THE EVENING THE WAITER COMES TO OUR TABLE WITH AN ENORMOUS BILL...

AND THIS WILL BE THE FIRST YEAR I WON'T BE ABLE TO USE GRANDAD'S PRESENT TO LIGHT MY AFTER-DINNER CIGAR.

MATCHES

Alex PEATTIE + TAYLOR

THAT OLD FRIEND YOU MET AT THE PARTY, WAS SHE REALLY ONCE "PLAYMATE OF THE MONTH" IN SOME PORN MAG?

OH... YES...

IT WAS VERY STUPID OF YOU TO MAKE MENTION OF IT IN FRONT OF ALL THOSE PEOPLE. IT WAS BOUND TO CAUSE EMBARRASSMENT...

I KNOW, I DIDN'T THINK...

THOUGH I MUST SAY I WAS SURPRISED TO HEAR ALL THOSE FEEBLE CLICHÉD JUSTIFICATIONS: "I WAS VERY YOUNG AT THE TIME; I DIDN'T REALLY KNOW WHAT I WAS DOING; I THOUGHT IT WOULD BE ARTISTIC; IT WAS JUST TOO TEMPTING..."

Peattie 239

SORRY BRIDGET, I WAS JUST GABBLING HYSTERICALLY...

...AND WHEN YOU CLAIMED THE "MAG" HAD BEEN DELIVERED BY MISTAKE INSTEAD OF "HOME COMPUTER WEEKLY..."